Backyard Books

Are you a Dragonfly?

For Kit—J. A.

For the Ladies of Holsworthy Library—T. H.

KINGFISHER
Larousse Kingfisher Chambers Inc.
95 Madison Avenue
New York, New York 10016
www.lkcpub.com

First published in 2001

1 3 5 7 9 10 8 6 4 2

1TR/0201/TWP/GRS/150NYM

LIBRARY OF CONGRESS CATALOGING-IN-PUBLICATION DATA
Allen, Judy.
Are you a dragonfly? / by Judy Allen; illustrated by Tudor Humphries.—1st ed.
p. cm.–(Backyard books)
ISBN 0-7534-5346-0
1. Dragonflies–Juvenile literature. [1. Dragonflies.] I. Humphries, Tudor ill. II. Title.

QL520 .A44 2001
595.7'33–dc21   00-048815

Editor: Carron Brown
Coordinating Editor: Laura Marshall
Series Designer: Jane Buckley

Printed in Singapore

Backyard Books

Are you a Dragonfly?

Judy Allen and Tudor Humphries

KING*f*ISHER

NEW YORK

Are you a dragonfly?

If you are, your mother
laid her eggs in
the stems of
water plants.

You swam out of one of them—and
so did lots of others just like you.

You are VERY small.

You are very hungry.

And guess what?
You can breathe water through
the end of your tail.

Eat and grow.

Eat tiny water creatures.

6

You have a special grabber for
catching them. It's called a mask
because it covers half your face.

Creep up on your prey—
then shoot out your mask
and grab it.

Eat and grow
until your skin
is so tight you
have to take it off.

Then eat and grow
some more, and do it again.

8

And again.

And again.

Don't worry, there will always be new skin underneath.

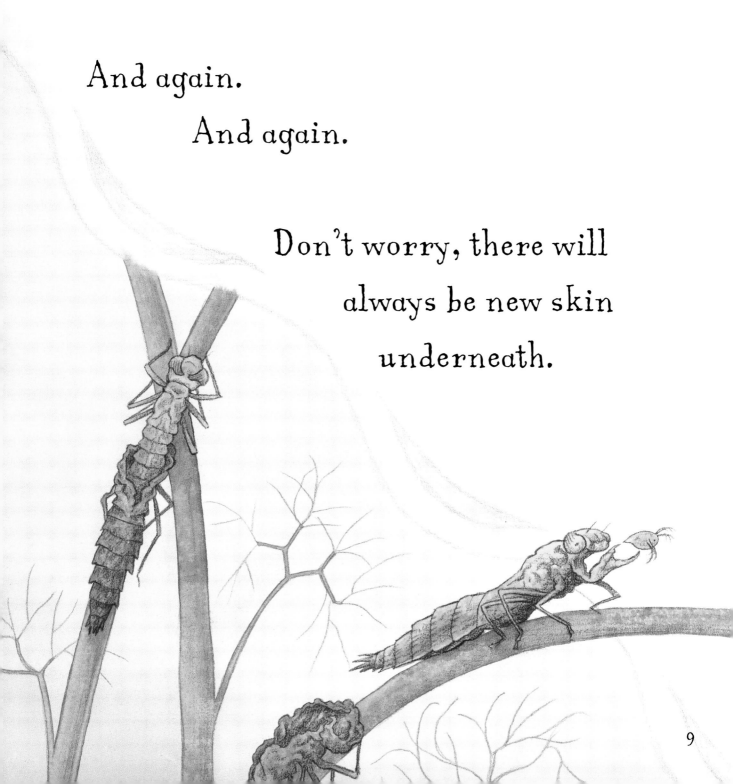

Now that you
have grown larger,
you can eat larger food.
Try a tadpole or a small fish.

But be careful—there are plenty
who would like to eat YOU.
Beware of water beetles.
Water beetles

p o u n c e !

Beware of ducks.
Ducks dive,
and they're
BIG.

Two years have passed. You're bored
with life in the water.

Crawl up a plant stem
into the air.

Do this at night so birds
don't see you and eat you.

Hold on tight. As you dry
your skin splits one more time.

13

Slowly, slowly,
climb out
of your
old skin.

First pull
your head free.
Then pull
your legs free.

Flop over backward
and have a rest.

14

Now lean forward, grab your old skin, and pull your whole body out.

Guess what? Now you can breathe air through tiny holes on the sides of your body.

15

You're a dragonfly!

At first you're very
pale and crumpled.

But your beautiful
colors will come, and
your two pairs of wings
will straighten out.

You're a fantastic flyer.

You can fly fast,

you can hover,

you can even
fly backward.

17

You have
enormous eyes.
You can see all
around you, all the time.

You can see what's behind you,
in front of you, above you,
below you, and beside you.

This is very useful
when you're looking for food.

This is also very useful when
you are dodging hungry birds
and avoiding spider's webs.

You were a fierce hunter
underwater—now you are
a fierce hunter in the air.

Hunt over ponds and streams
and slow-flowing rivers.
Hunt over marshes
and in forests.

Hold your legs out in front
of you to catch your prey.

Hunt midges and mosquitoes,
flies, wasps, and small butterflies.

When you catch
something, eat it.

You are a hawker—
you hunt while you're flying.

This dragonfly is a darter—
it sits still until it sees its prey,
then it darts out and grabs it.

This is not a dragonfly at all.
It's a damselfly. It's thinner and
lighter and slower than you.
It likes to pick small insects
off leaves and flowers.

Now look around you.
If you and all your friends look a little
like this

or this

or this

you are not a
dragonfly.

You are...

...a human child.

You can't fly.

You can't breathe
underwater.

It's very unlikely that you have
a mask attached to your face.

But you can do a lot of things
that dragonflies can't do.

You don't have to keep
taking your skin off,
and you don't have to eat
midges and mosquitoes.

Best of all, you'll never, ever, EVER be eaten by a duck.

Did You Know...

... there are more than 4,800 different kinds of dragonflies.

...dragonflies are among the oldest winged insects. They've been on the earth for about 300 million years— long before the dinosaurs.

...dragonflies have two pairs of wings. They can beat each pair separately, which is why they are such great flyers.

...dragonflies usually rest with their wings spread out, but damselflies usually fold their wings above their backs, the way butterflies do.